TINY HOUSE

BRENT HEAVENER

TINY HOUSE
LIVE SMALL, DREAM BIG

CLARKSON POTTER/PUBLISHERS
NEW YORK

CONTENTS

Introduction:
Find Freedom in Simplicity
6

1
Tree House Living
8

2
Eco-Friendly
32

3
Secluded Spaces
50

4
Family Home
94

5
High Up
110

6
Open Road
140

7
Down by the Water
174

8
Big Style, Small Home
196

Credits and Directory
246

FIND FREEDOM
IN SIMPLICITY

Imagine living free of the prescribed norms and daring to do it differently. No debt or mortgage to pay, no clutter and stuff to worry about and an environmentally friendly space to call your own that gives you boundless freedom. The widespread momentum of the tiny house movement has demonstrated that dream becoming a reality for people all over the world. Throughout the US, the UK, New Zealand, Australia and South Africa the shift towards a sovereign life free from financial bondage is growing and spreading globally. More and more creative individuals are pursuing a lifestyle with intention – a more balanced way to live that gives greater freedom and ultimately, more happiness.

As a kid in the mountains of California's high desert, some of my best adventures involved building forts in the trees or on the ground. Pieced together with scrap wood, bent nails and plywood, it was in these hideaways that I escaped chores and daily homeschooling. I could imagine, dream and allow my creativity to run wild. These imperfect walls were built from the heart – a battle cry of victory when I set the right board on, and sometimes tears when I hammered my thumb. The forts reflected something so much greater than what I knew at that time – they had character, determination and grit written all over them. They soothed the longing for

freedom and risk that lay within me as a young man.

Now, years later, that same desire for freedom is even greater and rings true to the hearts of so many others.

Visit a cosy cabin nestled in the Canadian wilderness, a renovated vintage van trekking through the American West, a whimsical tree house high in the forests of Spain, a mobile tiny house in the mountains of Washington or an A-frame atop Australia's golden hills. Whether you already live in a tiny house, are planning to build one or are simply seeking escapism, my hope is that a spark will be ignited upon the turning of each page.

Embark with me on this visual adventure as you journey through small spaces that inspire a passion to challenge the status quo and pursue a simpler life. A chance to get lost in your thoughts and dream of something more.

Venture ahead,

Brent

Brent Heavener is a digital entrepreneur, rancher and founder of @tinyhouse, the number one Tiny House feed on Instagram.

TREE HOUSE LIVING

BUILT UP HIGH IN SPAIN'S
BASQUE COUNTRY

Camouflaged among the fall leaves
of the trees, the octagon shape of
this home attracts those looking
for something special. A place to
step back from life and into nature,
to restore a sense of calm and an
appreciation of pared-back simplicity.

GRAND DOUBLE-DECKER TREE HOUSE RETREAT

Darin and Kati bought a seven-acre wooded property outside of Whitefish, Montana, and their dream of building a tree house became a reality. They created an unforgettable and grand escape within the trees. A winding staircase wraps around a salvaged Douglas Fir. The warm interior provides a comfortable space from which to admire the picturesque essence of the surrounding area. 'This whole project has been a true adventure in every sense of the word.'

A HIDEAWAY, CEDAR WOOD TREE HOUSE

Unique dwellings with rich character ingrained deep within them are few and far between. It takes a turn down an unknown road or a good word-of-mouth recommendation to find a place worth remembering. About an hour outside of Toronto, Frank and Oliver's tree house getaway on a 280-acre property is just like that. What started as an architectural project to build an unforgettable weekend retreat is now an escape to dwell and cherish moments within. Summer months are spent basking in the beauty around the lake, while the winter is taken up with visiting the local ski resorts to enjoy the slopes.

OPPOSITE
A BLOGGER'S ADVENTUROUS
HOME IN THE TREES

With her interior design skills in one hand, and knack for
giving reclaimed materials a second life in the other, Lynne
Knowlton had enough passion and coffee to fuel her long-
held tree house dream. Salvaged wood from an old barn
was used throughout and other foraged materials make this
characterful home unforgettably unique.

AN INCREDIBLE THREE-STOREY TREE HOUSE

At Camp Wandewega in Wisconsin, behind the reclaimed lumber and second-hand windows, lies an unforgettable space. It's rich with character and vintage finds. An elevated fireplace for those chilly northern nights and a lofted nook is the ideal place to relax and escape into a classic book.

OPPOSITE
ROTATING, HAND-CRANKED
MOUNTAIN TREE HOUSE

Up in the pines dwells an extraordinary rotating tree house. Ethan took his knack for creative engineering and built the system using parts from classic machines. He also gave some dead pine trees a second life by repurposing them in the interior. His inspiring home blends innovation with a simple, mountain essence, truly presenting a quintessential escape.

ECO-FRIENDLY

FINNISH SEASIDE SHELTER

Located on Vallisaari Island near Helsinki, Finland, lies the 'Nolla', a simple A-shaped structure that ties an eco-friendly vision with a minimal interior design. The concept was visualised and brought to life by Robin Falck, a Finnish industrial designer, and commissioned by Neste, a company focusing on sustainable solutions. The purpose – to create a home with a low impact on the environment that enabled the owner to dwell in complete freedom.

OFF-GRID GEODESIC DOME
IN PATAGONIA

Nestled between the grand snow-capped mountains of Torres del Paine, the EcoCamp Patagonia Domes offer a once-in-a-lifetime opportunity to experience the heart of Chile in its purest form. After a night of sleeping under the stars you'll wake up to a view of the nearby mountains, where wild alpacas graze on the slopes. Sip a traditional South American mate tea as you warm up next to the wood stove in this homey and unique dwelling.

STUNNING AUSTRALIAN
A-FRAME

Atop the golden hills of Australia's
Gundagai region dwells a modern
A-frame hut. Expansive views of the
7,000-acre working sheep and cattle
ranch from the home offer tranquillity
and wonder like no other. Bold in
design, innovative in structure and
exquisite in experience.

SECLUDED
SPACES

CHARMING AND NATURAL
SHEPHERD'S WAGON

Nestled between the pines of southern Quebec, this quaint
cabin is often the backyard to native deer and elk. With a
simple bed in one corner, a practical kitchen and a pot belly
wood stove to keep warm during those snowy winter nights,
the art of simple living is embodied in this quintessential
picturesque getaway. It's stress-proof, Walden-approved
and everything you've ever wanted.

HOMEY GETAWAY ON WHEELS

Buried within the woods of Massachusetts lies a dream
home, offering rest for those escaping a fast-paced city life,
or looking for some time away. Worries are left at the door
and there's no space for the 'stuff' of life to weigh you down
in this refreshing retreat. Simple living at its best allows the
beauty of the natural northeastern wildlife to shine.

LUXURY IN THE WOODS OF WISCONSIN

Buried in the Wisconsin woods is a mobile safe haven of shelter, providing a den of hibernation from the November snowfall. A full-sized window melts the barrier between outdoors and indoors, offering expansive views of all that the area has to offer. Simplistic, yet comfortable and functional, this home features a full-sized bed to rest in, allowing a place to appreciate the beauty of the natural surroundings.

TEXAN CRAFTSMAN'S RAW AND ROLLING HOME

Brett Lewis' passion for creating
inspiring spaces began when he
searched Craigslist for his next
project. With grit and determination
he set about transforming an old
'86 Vanagon into a vintage rolling
home named 'Chewy'. The majority
of Chewy's one-of-a-kind renovated
interior is made from salvaged
Texas cedar.

HAND-BUILT TENT CABIN IN MAINE

Deep in the woods of Maine's Acadia National Park lies an eclectic dwelling fit for those who yearn for a quintessential, unconventional escape. The 'Coyotes Den' is not a typical cabin tent. The love for the heritage of the structure is apparent in the craftsmanship throughout and the respect given to nature invites the dweller to slow down and pay homage to what once was. Its owners had a goal, 'to share all the little things that make this life special to us. It's a place to live simply and in harmony with the woods of Maine.'

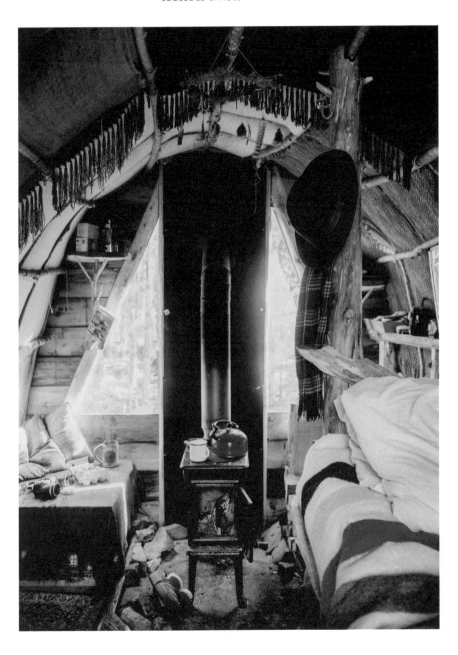

A COSY A-FRAME IN THE MOUNTAINS OF WASHINGTON

Hidden within the towering pines
of Washington rests a quaint and
picturesque A-frame. Built in 1965,
but newly remodelled, the A-frame
combines a rich cabin interior feel
with minimal elements, making it an
ideal sanctuary in the woods. Mount
Rainier is a short commute away,
while the Nisqually river is only a
few steps out the back door.

REPURPOSED AND ELEGANT
SHIPPING CONTAINER

Imagine waking up in a renovated shipping container, walking outside and up your steps and taking in the crisp morning air from a rooftop deck. This tiny container house, built by a family-owned business from Waco, Texas, focuses on transforming containers into elegant and efficient homes. Practical design and thoughtful craftsmanship collide in creating a beautiful space that bridges indoor living with the outdoors.

BOLD SCANDINAVIAN-STYLE DWELLING

Designed by Fernando Morrisoniesko, this modern rustic dwelling embodies a lifestyle of intentionality towards indoors and outdoors. The 'Refuge' is designed to be nestled between evergreen pines in the Sonoran mountain range of Mexico. Thoughtfully bridging indoor living with nature, being mindful of what's important in life comes with no difficulty in this space. Inspired by Scandinavian architecture, it touts bold design aspects with its core grounded in minimalism. It's an ideal place to write or a much-needed escape. When I look upon this space, I see something more than a well-designed area for living. The concept of a home is grander than four walls and a roof. A place to dwell, in all its purity, is an art form, relaying conversation from the past, experiences only known by the artist and emotions that are bound to develop into their intended creation.

FAMILY
HOME

DOWNSIZING LIFE TO AN
UPGRADED AIRSTREAM

After Zach had unexpected brain
surgery in 2013, he and his wife,
Colleen, looked around and noticed
how short life could be. They had a
wake-up call and saw the way they
were living life just wasn't right,
so Zach with his experience in
construction and Colleen with her love
for design, renovated an Airstream
into a home for their two boys. Their
home provides a light and minimal
atmosphere, with custom touches
and hand-picked, reclaimed finds.
Living in a tiny house has given them
the opportunity to start a business
of renovating Airstreams for others
looking to live minimally.

A HIDDEN FAMILY ESCAPE

The Ruiz family embody an authentic life of simplicity and free living that few come across. Resting in the high desert of New Mexico and nestled between willow trees lies their handmade, creative and inspiring tent. With the right design and a little ingenuity, you don't need a lot of money to make a space look stunning. Featuring an industrial metal and reclaimed wood table, and handmade light fixtures from rope and metal, their home shows that a little intentional design goes a long way. They wake up every day to raw, untouched nature and the simple things that add to their joy. With head and heart poured into their homestead, they've founded a 'den for our cubs' in the forest.

A ROLLING HOME WITH HAPPINESS AHEAD

Buying a bus, renovating it and making the open road your home is a dream that's spoken of by many, but done by few. Meet Ben and Mande, who took that dream and made it a reality. After searching for just the right bus to convert into their full-time home, they came across a classic school one. They worked on it every day until their fully functional, spacious and well-designed home on wheels was complete. 'We stayed motivated by dreaming of the upcoming adventures she'd bring us on. We knew she'd introduce us to new people and places, and shake us out of our routines and habits.' Since then, they've conquered the open roads of the West, been on a number of exciting adventures and have added a new member to the crew: their son Sawyer. With a passion for adventure and the outdoors, they're living the life of simplicity and freedom that they've always dreamed of.

FAMILY ADVENTURE ON THE OPEN ROAD

Meet Mars, Ashley and their daughter Everly, who went from a four-bedroom house to a renovated Sprinter van. They're able to live with less and spend more of their life around what they love. Their van, called 'Edison', packs big features into a small home. A pull-out deck built from reclaimed pallets serves as a spot to lie down or as a picnic table. When they've stopped off for the night after travelling into the mountains or down to the beach, their rooftop deck offers expansive views of the midnight stars and incredible Milky Way. Their multi-functional use of space shows just how much you can do. When asked what advice Ashley would give to someone looking to go tiny, she said 'With a smaller home, a smaller budget can go way further than you might think. Get creative. Brainstorm. Most of all, have FUN.'

CUSTOM-DESIGNED CREATIVE LIVING
IN NORTHERN CALIFORNIA

Joshua and Shelley were able to take what they learned from living tiny and start a business selling trailers, write a book and help folks who are interested in moving into a smaller home. Their self-built house resonates that message, that when it comes to building your tiny home, the possibilities are endless. You don't need to be confined to the latest 'trend' or even your own self-created limitations. A tiny home is the canvas and you're the artist.

CONTEMPORARY, JOY-FILLED MOTORHOME

Meet the Petrones, a family of five from Southern
California, who took an old motorhome and converted
it into a stunning, but functional and inviting house on
wheels. Ashley put her own sense of design to work, adding
a black and white tile backsplash, butcher block worktops
and small contemporary touches that made a big difference.
In the end, their temporary home, while they built a new
one, created a long-lasting change within them, 'So while
we moved into the trailer thinking it would be for a few
months, it ended up being a journey that we loved and
really changed our lives.'

HIGH UP

MODERN MOBILE DWELLING
IN CALIFORNIA'S MOUNTAINS

With no major previous experience in construction, this home is a testament to this couple's leap of faith towards a more content, decluttered life. It's a remarkable story of moving into a more intentional space for increased freedom without a big bank account to fund the build. The interior's industrial, modern and simplistic vibe provides ample storage solutions for a small space. Birch veneer plywood was used for the flooring, cabinets, ceiling and walls, while outside is clad in cedar siding, with one side behind higher than the other, creating a structure that reflects a unique architectural design.

A PLACE OF SANCTUARY

Grab your favourite blanket, hot cocoa and bunker down in this double-lofted, picturesque cabin. With nature as your neighbour and a sound structure of natural materials as your shelter, finding rest comes with ease. Days are spent outside appreciating the natural wildlife, while chilly evenings are taken up around the centrally located fireplace enjoying good laughs and cabin-cooked meals. I must say, though, that the best times are those finding sanctuary in the loft, deep in a good book, covered in handmade quilts for an extra layer of warmth.

MODERN SUSTAINABLE
HAWAIIAN HIDEOUT

Situated among the lush tropical flora, the Outside House,
a two-structured home, provides a unique escape to the
untouched Hawaiian ecosystem. The open pavilion named
'Makai', consists of an outdoor kitchen and shower, creating
a life outside of four walls. Nearby lies the 'Mauka', a small
cabin with rich elements of wood ideal for writing and resting.

MINIMALIST SLEEK DESIGN IN
THE WASHINGTON MOUNTAINS

Hidden in the basket of the Washington mountains this retreat is girded with a steel frame and clad with an interior of simplistic pine plywood. The Rolling Hut offers shelter for one, seeking what's necessary for a life of purpose and tranquillity. Located in Mazama, Washington, the simple hut provides a low-impact, mindful escape into nature. The innovative architecture sets the pace for solace as you dwell within it, aiding in the quest for an inner peace and a lifestyle of contentment.

OPEN ROAD

TRAVELLING NORWAY AND BEYOND

When they aren't trekking up snow-capped mountains in Europe, or venturing down vast stretches of road in South East Asia, Ann-Sylvia and Georg are back home in Norway restoring their energy for their next creative project. After travelling over an expanse of countries, these two artists, photographers and filmmakers embarked on a journey in their van from Norway to India, documenting eco-entrepreneurs on the way. Living a lifestyle that's different from those around them and taking the unbeaten path inspires their art and feeds their adventurous souls.

WORLD-TRAVELLER, RISK-TAKER
AND TRENDSETTER

There are not many people out there quite like James Barkman. At 21, he bought a 1976 Volkswagen Westfalia, furthering an authentic and spontaneous lifestyle in pursuit of his passions. He's surfed swells along the American West Coast, conquered the Pan-American Highway from Alaska to Patagonia via motorcycle and photo-documented vivid moments in rarely travelled regions. He's been through a number of motorcycles, but currently keeps his 1984 Honda XR350R by his side to trek through tough places his van isn't able to travel. Through it all, it's been faithful to take him to wherever he wants to explore. 'So far I haven't been able to tell if she leaks more oil than she burns, or burns more oil than she leaks.'

EXPLORING ONWARD IN AN
'88 CUSTOM-BUILT VINTAGE VAN

Imagine a life roaming the open road and seeking
adventure in a custom-designed, 1988 Chevy Sportvan.
Welcome to Candice's life. In 2014, Candice, a creative and
adventurous woman, decided to leave her conventional
way of life for freedom, happiness and simplicity. With no
past experience in building, she created a unique home
on wheels that offers a warm and rustic atmosphere. She
thoughtfully designed simple solutions to everyday needs by
not wasting any space. With a free-spirited soul ambitious
for adventure, she'll continue to conquer the open road and
make memories wherever her travels may take her.

LIFE ON THE ROAD WITH A CAMERA,
A SURFBOARD AND TRUTH AS HIS GUIDE

Behind the wheel of a 1978 Volkswagen Westfalia you'll find a bearded, eccentric nomad who lives by the beat of his own drum. Meet Daniel Norris, the major league baseball pitcher who spends his offseason living out of his camper van in search of surf and unknown destinations off the beaten path, spurred on by a curiosity of the world around him. The status quo doesn't confine him, conformity is his antithesis and life's curveballs don't dismay him. 'I'm in search of three things,' Norris says, 'eternal life, the strike zone, and good waves.'

ADVENTURE FROM
ALASKA TO ARGENTINA

Skating down the desert roads of El
Chalten, Argentina, hiking snow-
capped mountains in Alaska and
fishing off the coasts of Mexico, Dillon
and Tessa can tell of these adventures
because they stepped outside the
lifestyle that came with normality and
chose freedom to the fullest. They
bought a classic 1976 VW Westfalia,
fitted it with a Subaru engine and set
off into the unknown. They ventured
from their home state of Alaska down
to Argentina, then back to Alaska.
Dillon and Tessa's authentic travels
and fearless ambition inspire the soul
not to overthink how your dream will
be accomplished, but to step outside
your comfort zone. 'When people tell
us they wish they were able to live
the lifestyle that we chose we always
remind them that we are just a few
dishevelled "goobers" that decided
to take the plunge. If you're feeling
the need for change, listen to your
intuition and take the leap! The first
mile is the hardest.'

A HEART FOR THE FRONTIER

Forging new paths, roaming the open road and
reaching new peaks are just a few things that are
a part of the adventurous and eccentric lifestyle of
young pioneer, Trey Frye. At 18, he bought a 1986 VW van
and hit the open road with his faithful Belgian Malinois and
Smith & Wesson model 10 .38 by his side. His drive for
authentic creativity keeps him rolling down a spontaneous
and adventurous path. When he's found a good spot to
camp for the night, he'll prepare his van or tent for sleeping
and make a fire. You'll often find him waking up early to
trek up a mountain to capture the morning sun. Currently
he's on the West Coast with a camera and a '90 Yamaha
xt350 hitched to the back of his van.

SMART, MODERN AND MOBILE

After travelling the world, Dominic and Marie decided to bridge their love for exploration with their jobs. In the summer of 2018, together with their families, they renovated this van into their own stunning mobile home and office. A uniform style of clean, white walls accented by the rich craftsmanship of the wood floors, ceiling and countertops creates a remarkable interior design. The two large back doors open up the home to the view of wherever they've travelled, offering a fluid transition between the indoors and outdoors.

FINDING FREEDOM ON THE ROAD

I first had the chance to meet Ben and Meag in mid-2018. Their warm personalities, joy and passion to educate others on the benefits of intentional and healthy living have stuck with me over time. In 2013, after acquiring a lot of debt, they knew something needed to happen. Fast-forward to December 2017: debt-free, they quit their jobs and embarked on an unforgettable journey in their 1989 renovated prison bus. Now on the road, the summer months are spent basking in the beauty that New Hampshire's White Mountains have to offer, while winters are spent in the dry heat of the Southwest. Rich in character and seasoned with hand-picked finds, their home could easily be called a museum on wheels. By not going the route of buying traditional furniture, they added their own unique style and signature by making it all from scratch. 'Our home is a unique reflection of us. Every inch is Ben and Meag. I look around and see our love, ability to problem solve, compromise, prioritise and create. It is as stubborn as we are, no shortcuts taken.'

TWO PHOTOGRAPHERS AND
THE GREAT OUTDOORS

Around the towering pines of the Pacific northwest, up the rocks of Moah, Utah and through the desert of Arizona, Kyle and Jodie have explored it all in their 1955 Flying Cloud Airstream. Renovated with a clean and rich look, their Airstream includes the perfect-sized kitchen and a built-in mini fireplace for those colder locations. Together with their dogs, they've found freedom by escaping a life of mundanity in exchange for the open road and endless inspiration. They spend their time exploring new destinations, meeting with other people living alternatively and furthering their passion for creativity through photography and film-making.

TRAVELS IN A RENOVATED MOTORHOME

Meet Pauline and Kieran from Australia who were saving up for two dreams: either buying a house or going on a trip overseas. After coming to the realisation that they could bridge the two, they decided to travel to the States and live in a home on wheels, taking a 'mental gap year'. What followed was two weeks of completely transforming the old space into a new, stylish and rustic-chic home, then months of peaceful travels through North America's wonders and natural beauty.

DOWN BY
THE WATER

HOUSEBOAT LIVING ON AUSTRALIA'S NOOSA RIVER

I remember as a kid the classic Mark Twain story *The Adventures of Huckleberry Finn*. As a young boy, spending your days on a handmade house raft with only the moon for light at night was something only dreamed of. Not as basic as Huck's, pictured is a houseboat on Australia's Noosa River. No matter the size or complexity, there's just something about living on the water. Going with the pace of the river around you seems to spark a curiosity within the hearts of those that seek this kind of floating, peaceful and simple lifestyle.

CREEKSIDE IN CALIFORNIA

No to-do lists, schedules or appointments to interrupt the atmosphere of the Far Meadow A-frame. The only meeting planned is between you and nature. Situated in the Sierra Nevada's, California, it's a favourite getaway for those in need of a rest and recharge.

A SIMPLE WATERFRONT COTTAGE

Imagine yourself off the coast of Sweden gazing upon
your humble home for the night. The smell of saltwater
and fresh pines fill the atmosphere as you sail towards the
cliffs the house dwells upon. Inside the walls of the small
cottage lies your shelter, a place of comfort and solitude.
A cup of tea brewed from herbs from the nearby forest
awaits you as it finds warmth on the fireplace. Pictures of
memories fill the walls. Shelves and coffee tables are the
home of books on architecture, home-making and bird
species found in that region. The light elements of the
Scandinavian design creates a welcoming and inviting
atmosphere. Functionality and comfort collide in creating
your dream summer getaway.

WAKE UP ON THE BEACH
IN THIS CUSTOM-DESIGNED
FAMILY HOME

The Tillmans always knew they
wanted to live tiny. They're both
photographers, so their dream was
to be able to create a life where they
could travel and work at the same
time. Off they embarked, remodelling
a motorhome into a stunning rustic,
industrial and modern little house on
wheels. It's got everything they need
to live and work comfortably without
breaking their budget. 'We built for
our needs. It's not perfect, but I have
even come to love all of the little
imperfections.'

BIG STYLE, SMALL HOME

ZERO-WASTE, MINIMALISM
AND COMFORT IN THIS TEXAN HOME

Airy, inviting and a happy atmosphere – that's how I'd describe Canaan and Kelly's Texas tiny home. After coming to the realisation of how much 'stuff' they had acquired, going tiny attracted them. To make the transition to a simpler life, they downsized to their current 312-square foot (29-square metre) tiny house. The overall spacious design and functional layout set the home apart. They both have different interior design tastes, but were able to meet in the middle to create an inviting space with elegant tones and farmhouse elements.

A YOUNG COUPLE'S DREAM

It all started one evening while Cody
and Shay were at a restaurant. For
a while they had tossed around the
ridiculous and absolutely radical idea
of building a tiny house. Then, it hit
them. 'Wait a minute, why are we
talking about this like it's something
extremely unrealistic, or a completely
out of reach dream?'

Fast-forward six months, $23k
and a baby on the way, they stood
looking at their tiny home. Once a
dream, now a reality. Their home
boasts spaciousness and functionality,
including a double loft, large kitchen
and essential storage space. There's
no end to the incredible features
within it. Often a dream that seems
unrealistic, impossible and almost
crazy (a bit wild), is exactly the thing
you should do. Cody and Shay stopped
talking about their dream, and started
working towards it. 'Most important
of all, we learned that anything is
possible. We had a dream and we
made it a reality. WE BUILT A
TINY HOUSE!'

HANDMADE AND HUMBLE

As an artist, collector and maker, New Zealander Lily's
home is a rendition of who she is, reflecting her pure sense
of originality and character. Each piece within its four
walls has a story of its own, hand-picked and cherished by
Lily herself. Furniture, china, books and stained glass with
a rich history, revived and living a second life peacefully
alongside each other. In the end, what a makes a home is
living surrounded by what you love.

OPPOSITE
AN AUTHOR'S PEACEFUL RETREAT

Matt, from HandCrafted Movement, turned a vision into a reality for Ann Voskamp, her husband and her family. Tucked away in the woods, it has become a place where words flow, rest resounds and the worries of the day are left at the door. 'We name this tiny house Selah because Selah means "silence" or "pause". We say it all the time: "slipping out to the Selah…" And even that phrase feels like a soul exhale: we are slipping away to pause and still and listen to the silence so we can hear joy loudest in our souls.'

OPPOSITE
COLOMBIA CRAFTSMAN

An immaculate house designed and built by Matt Impola
and his team, near Portland, Oregon.

ABOVE
PACIFIC HARMONY

Marked by their cohesive styling and inclusion of salvaged
wood, every home envisioned and made a reality by Matt
Impola and his team showcases a passionate skill for the
art. The 'Pacific Harmony' is an elegantly crafted house,
near Portland, Oregon, that features solid oak flooring,
stainless steel appliances and a murphy bed. The fine
details and personally sourced materials throughout give an
overall sense of 'home'.

RISK-TAKING, GO-GETTING EMPTY NESTERS

John and Val knew that they needed to blaze a new trail once their four homeschooled kids had left the nest. With determination and a little bit of faith, they went for it and built a home in British Columbia, Canada, on a small plot of land, with everything they need for a simple life.

OFF-GRID VERSATILE INGENUITY

To go beyond the limits of the status quo and do the out-of-the-ordinary is the heart of what makes up the tiny house lifestyle. Wohnwagon, an Austrian design and home building team, is creating tiny homes on wheels that embody just that. They've taken the visual concept of tiny living to a new level with sleek, rounded corners, a double-axle trailer and a European style flourishing throughout every small detail within the home. Their picturesque houses are ideal for simple living.

ABOVE
CALIFORNIA MAKER'S SELF-BUILT SPACE

Living in a tiny house is not for the ordinary in heart, spirit or action. This lifestyle, and everything it offers, makes a common connection within those desiring to rise out of where they are into a life of freedom. This takes determination. Shalina, Sacramento maker, designer and collector, who designed and built her own tiny house, lived out just that.

OPPOSITE
SIMPLE LIVING

Before she downsized, Dolly, a cook, photographer and IT engineer, was living in a high-rise apartment in the fast-paced city of Melbourne, Australia. After getting a taste of the tiny house lifestyle by staying in funky vans and eclectic structures, she was infatuated. Fast-forward to now, and she's happily living in her self-designed tiny house on a 420-acre farm. Her home has everything she wants – a spacious kitchen to cook food for her blog, a composting toilet for minimising waste and even a walk-in wardrobe!

GRAND, IMPECCABLE AND INNOVATIVE

Designed and built out of Nashville, Tennessee, the timeless design and fine craftsmanship of this tiny dream home creates a one-of-a-kind piece of art. It sets itself apart by boasting unique storage options, a raised stunning kitchen and natural, rustic tones. Outdoor nature and indoor living collide by opening up the heart of the home using the large glass garage door.

STUNNING EXCEPTIONALLY DESIGNED HOME

Overlooking the Santa Cruz Mountains is the luxurious home of a Northern Californian young couple and their two-and-a-half-year-old daughter. After spending $30k on a year's rent in a Bay Area apartment in San Francisco, they knew they needed to invest their money with intentionality and creativity. Going beyond the boundaries of the norm for a standard tiny house, their home not only packs beauty, style and functionality into a few hundred square feet, making the most of the money they've spent, it also doubles as a lucrative cash flow by being used for short-term rentals while they travel. When you have a purpose and a plan with your money, and are willing to ride out the bumps as they come, living in a tiny house doesn't seem so bad, huh?

LITTLE FARMHOUSE ON WHEELS

This tiny home, clad with cedar exterior siding, resides within the natural, wild and untouched mountainous California terrain. Inside, the home creates an inviting and light atmosphere by balancing white shiplap on the walls with natural wood textures and a built-in fireplace. What sets this home apart is the unique spacious bathroom rare to most tiny homes. The large, round window adds the perfect touch by illuminating the atmosphere with natural, warm light.

CREDITS AND DIRECTORY

COVER

Front cover: Nolla: Sustainable A-Frame near Helsinki, Finland. © Joonas Linkola.

Back cover: Vantage Tiny Home: Built by Tiny Heirloom out of Portland, Oregon. © Tiny Heirloom.

PRELIMS

p.2 Nolla: Sustainable A-Frame near Helsinki, Finland. © Joonas Linkola.

p.4 Lynne Knowlton's Cabin Retreat: Well-designed light cabin near Toronto, Canada. © Lynne Knowlton | TreeHouse & Cabin Retreat.

p.7 A-frame: Idyllic escape in the Alaskan mountains, USA. © Mark Reyes/Naanod.jpg.

TREE HOUSE LIVING

p.10–12 Tree House: 55 feet up in the trees of Spain. © Leire Unzueta.

p.13 Montana Tree House Retreat: Grand double-decker just outside of Whitefish, Montana, USA. © Kati O'Toole.

p.14–15 Fox House: Tree house built with reclaimed windows in Nashville, Tennessee, USA. © Laura Dart/ The Fox House by Emily Leonard Southard and Sloane Southard.

p.17 Tree House: Built from cedar, near Toronto, Canada. © Suech and Beck.

p. 18–19, 21, 23 Lynne Knowlton's Tree House: Constructed from reclaimed materials near Toronto, Canada.

© Lynne Knowlton | TreeHouse & Cabin Retreat.

p.20, 22 Lynne Knowlton's Cabin Retreat: Well-designed light cabin near Toronto, Canada. © Lynne Knowlton | TreeHouse & Cabin Retreat.

p.24–25 Tree House at Camp Wandawega: Three-storey tree house built around an elm tree in the woods of Wisconsin, USA. © Bennett Young.

p.26–27 Characterful wooden tree house. © Suech and Beck.

p.28 Cabin tucked away in the woods of Oregon. © Bennett Young.

p.29 The Lushna Cabin. © Connor Willgress/Lushna Cabin at Eastwind Hotel & Bar Windham, NY.

p.30 Ethan incredible bicycle-powered tree house in the USA. © Mikey Gribbin.

p.31 Ethan Tree House: Two-storey hand-cranked tree house that rotates 360°, in the mountains, USA. © Mikey Gribbin.

ECO-FRIENDLY

p.34–35 Nolla: Sustainable A-Frame near Helsinki, Finland. © Joonas Linkola.

p.36–39 EcoCamp Patagonia: Sustainable Geodesic domes, mountains of Torres Del Paine, Chile. © Sasha Juliard.

p.40–41 Hideout Bali: Sustainable eco retreat in Bali, Indonesia. © Sasha Juliard.

p.42–45 Kimo Estate: Modern off-grid A-Frame overlooking the Gundagai hills, Australia. © Nicole Clark Photography.

p.46–47 Glass house built from salvaged windows and reclaimed materials in the woods of West Virginia, USA. © Nick Olson.

p.48 Picturesque Pod in Great Britain. © Calin Gillespie.

p.49 Cabin retreat within the Elmley Nature Reserve on an island off the coast of Great Britain. © Kym Grimshaw/Elmley Nature Reserve.

SECLUDED SPACES

p.52–55 Kayak Café: Shepherd's wagon in southern Quebec, Canada. © Dominic Faucher | VanLife Sagas.

p.56–57 A-Frame: Rustic home © Brendan Lynch.

p.58 Loft: © Brendan Lynch.

p.59 Getaway House: Tiny house rental in the woods of Massachusetts, USA. © Heather Sorrenty.

p.60–61 Sunlit Shanti at Pegasus Farm, near Mendocino, California, USA. © Bennett Young.

p.62–63 Vista: A mobile safe haven of shelter, woods of Wisconsin, USA. © ESCAPE RV/Steve Niedorf.

p.64–65 Brett Lewis' 1986 Vanagon: Renovated with salvaged Texas cedar, Texas, USA. © Ventana Media Collective.

p.66 Cabinscape's Mason Cabin: A well-designed escape situated on 576 acres in Southern Ontario, Canada. © Evelyn Barkey Photography.

p.68–71 Coyotes Den: Hand-built tent cabin at Howling Woods, Acadia National Park, Maine, USA. © Max Ablicki.

p.72–75 Desert Yurt: A simplistic yurt surrounded by extraordinary terrain in Utah USA. © Sasha Juliard.

p.76–77 Candlewood Cabin's Glass House: A peaceful retreat in the woods of Wisconsin, USA. © Peter Godshall.

p.78–79 Hebe's Hideout: Remodelled 1965 A-Frame near Mt Rainier, Washington, USA. © Shon Purdy.

p.80 Cabin with character, USA. © Kyle Finn Dempsey | YouTube: trout and coffee.

p.81 Off-grid cabin rental, Vermont, USA. © Kyle Finn Dempsey | YouTube: trout and coffee.

p.82 Container tiny home: Shipping container with rooftop deck, based in Texas, USA. © Alexis McCurdy.

p.84–85 Rustic Caravan: a vintage, creative escape in California, USA. © Bennett Young.

p.86–87 Home of Zen: Built by Tiny Heirloom out of Portland, Oregon. © Tiny Heirloom.

p.88–89 Library cabin. © Lennart Pagel.

p.90–91 Vantage Tiny Home: Built by Tiny Heirloom out of Portland, Oregon. © Tiny Heirloom.

p.92–93 Refuge: Scandinavian-inspired rustic small space in the Sonoran Mountain Range, Mexico. © Fernando Morrisoniesko.

FAMILY HOME

p.96–97 Cashio's Airstream: Renovated 1972 airstream for family, Arkansas, USA. © Sydney Sligh Photography.

p.98–99 Den for our cubs: Secluded family tent escape in the high desert of New Mexico, USA. © Zachary Ruiz.

p.100 Fern the Bus: Renovated school bus serving as the home for an adventurous young family. © Ben & Mande Tucker.

p.101 Open tiny home built by Tiny Life Construction. © Tiny Life Construction.

p.102–105 Fite Travels: Renovated Sprinter van. © Sami Strong Photography.

p.106–107 Joshua and Shelley's House: Custom-designed, self-built home with a view, Northern California, USA. © Joshua Engberg/Tiny House Basics.

p.108–109 The Petrones: Airy, contemporary home on wheels in Southern California, USA. © Ashley Petrone.

HIGH UP

p. 112–113 Cabin in the woods, North America © Dominic Faucher | VanLife Sagas"

p.115 Log Wood Cabin. © Brendan Lynch.

p.116 Omah Kayu. © Abraham Yusuff.

p.117 Mountain-top small dwelling, Sweden. © Sasha Juliard.

p.118–119 Black A-Frame. © Brendan Lynch.

p.120 Cabin getaway in Austria. © Michael Derjabin

p.121 Cabin retreat in Austria © Roman Huber.

p.122–125 Woody Tiny House: Modern mobile dwelling, mountains of California, USA. © Benjamin Rasmussen Photo.

p.126–127 Tye Haus A-Frame: Cabin rental in the Washington mountains, USA. © Bennett Young.

p.128 Incredibly designed small structure in Italy. © Joonas Linkola.

p.129 Quaint homey cabin. © Chris Daniele.

p.130 Heart of it all House: Trevor Gay's tiny home. © Trevor Gay/Strayer Media.

p.131–133 Raven House: Off-grid cabin getaway, Ontario, Canada. © Chris Daniele.

p.134–137 Outside House: Modern and sustainable two-structured build on a 300 year old Hawaiian lava flow, Hawaii, USA. © Olivier Koning.

p.138–139 Rolling Hut: Minimalist steel frame and plywood retreat, mountains of Mazama, Washington, USA. © Tim Bies/Olson Kundig.

OPEN ROAD

p.142–147 Ann-Sylvia & Georg Deocariza: Creative couple's 1980 VW LT 31 home on wheels Norway and beyond. © Georg & Ann-Sylvia Deocariza.

p. 148–151 James Barkman: Photographer and traveller's authentic 1976 VW Westfalia van with mini wood stove, USA. © James Barkman.

p.152–155 Candice Smith: Custom-built vintage 1988 Chevy Sportvan, USA. © Candice Smith.

p.156–157 Daniel Norris: Surfer and photographer's 1978 VW Westfalia on the open road, USA. © Ben Moon.

p.158–159 The Bus and Us: Couple's converted C1976 VW Westfalia van, Alaska, USA. © That Feeling Co/The Bus And Us.

p.160–161 Trey Frye: Young photographer's 1986 VW Van, venturing the open road, USA. © Trey Frye.

p.162–163 Van Life Sagas: Renovated van into mobile home and office, Quebec, Canada. © Dominic Faucher/VanLife Sagas.

p.164–165 Wild Drive Life: Prison bus transformed into home on wheels. © Rachel Halsey Photography/Wild Drive Life.

p. 166–171 Brisk Venture: Photographer's 1955 Flying Cloud Airstream on the road, USA. © Kyle Murphy/Brisk Venture.

p.172–173 Pauline Morrissey: Stylish and rustic-chic motorhome, travelled through North America, USA. © Pauline Morrissey.

DOWN BY THE WATER

p.176–177 Houseboat: Simple houseboat living on the Noosa River, Australia. © Levi Caleb Allan.

p.178–179 Red cabin on the water, Europe. © Joonas Linkola.

p.180–181 Red Lake House: Island house by the water, Europe. © Joonas Linkola.

p.183 Cabin on the water: Austria. © Sebastian Scheichl.

p.184–185 Far Meadow House: Rustic, modern creekside A-frame rental near Yosemite, California, USA. © Laura Austin.

p.186–187 Timbercraft: Denali Tiny Home in Alabama, USA. © Patrick Oden.

p.188–189 Waterfront cottage in Sweden, Europe. © Olga Redina.

p.190–191 Das Bååt: Floating wooden cabin at Naturbyn, Sweden. © Juila This.

p.192–195 Tillman motorhome: Rustic, industrial modern house on wheels, USA. © The Tillmans.

BIG STYLE, SMALL HOME

p.198–201 Alek's Lisefski's Tiny House: Sustainable, self-built home on wheels, Sonoma Valley, California, USA. © Thomas J. Story/Sunset Publishing Corp.

p.202–205 Golden House: Zero-waste, minimalist, yet comfortable home, Texas, USA. © Kelly Christine Sutton.

p. 206–207 Eclectic, well-designed tiny home with vintage pieces, USA. © Apartment Therapy/Carina Romano.

p.208 Modern Cottage: Pine-clad, space-saving getaway in the Pyrenees Mountains, Spain. © José Hevia.

p.209 Rowan's Tiny Home: Elegant craftsmanship in this New York home, USA. © Deborah DeGraffenreid.

p.210–211 Cody Woodworth's Tiny Home: Spacious and functional space for small family USA. © Cody Woodworth/321 Explore.

p.212 Bill and Beck Shepherd's Hut: Timber built shepherd's hut in the hills of Wales, Great Britain. © Rustic Campers.

p.213 Indigo: luxurious tiny home from in Brighton, South Carolina, USA. © Tom Jenkins/Brighton Builders SC.

p.215 Lily Duval's Tiny Home: Handmade and humble home in New Zealand. © Jane Ussher, *NZ House & Garden*.

p.216 Farmhouse Tiny Home: Elegant, skilfully crafted home, built in Lancaster, Pennsylvania, USA. © Liberation Tiny Homes.

p.217 Selah Studio: Peaceful retreat for author and speaker Ann Voskamp, North America. © Matt Impola.

p.218 Colombia Craftsman: Spacious, articulately-designed home near Portland, Oregon, USA. © Matt Impola.

p.219 Pacific Harmony: Salvaged wood and cohesive styling, near Portland, Oregon, USA. © Matt Impola.

p.220 Mint Rustic: Style and natural materials, British Columbia, Canada. © James Alfred Photography.

p.221 Great Canadian Tiny House: Empty nester's simple, small living, Canada. © James Alfred Photography.

p.222–223 Wohnwagon: Off-grid, versatile homes on wheels, Austria. © Wohnwagon GmbH.

p.224 The Laurier: Minimalist comfort with floor-level bedroom in Quebec, Canada. © Minimaliste Houses.

p.225 Wandering On Wheels: Self-built escape from corporate life, Colorado. © Barry Sanford/Wandering On Wheels.

p.226 Shalina Kell's House: Self-designed, functional living space, Sacramento. © Shalina Kell/Her Tiny Home.

p.227 Miss Dolly: Self-designed and simple, set on a cattle, sheep and chicken farm in Australia. © Dolly Rubiano.

p.228–231 The Alpha: Tiny house with an innovative design and craftsmanship, Nashville, Tennessee, USA. © Designed and built by David Latimer/New Frontier Tiny Homes | Photos by Studio Buell Photography.

p.232 The Orchid: Modern, minimal tiny house design, out of Nashville, Tennessee, USA. © Designed and built by David Latimer/New Frontier Tiny Homes | Photos by Studio Buell Photography.

p.233–237 Bela Fishbeyn: Beauty, style and functionality in the Santa Cruz Mountains, California, USA. © Bela Fishbeyn.

p.238–241 Greenmoxie: Tiny home with a sustainable focus, Canada. © Nikki Fotheringham/ Greenmoxie.

p.242–243 Little farmhouse on wheels, California, USA. © Dillan Forsey.

p.244–245 Colton Ronzio: Extraordinary design and use of raw materials in South Carolina, USA. © Danny Zarate.

CREDITS AND DIRECTORY

p.247 Lynne Knowlton's tiny house: © Lynne Knowlton | TreeHouse & Cabin Retreat.

p.248 Ryan's Tiny House: Handmade from salvaged materials, Idaho, USA. © Brittany Bunker Photography.

p.251 Small mountain home: Mountains of Boone, North Carolina, USA. © John D. Stephens / That Hiker.

p.252 Lynne Knowlton's Tree House: Constructed from reclaimed materials near Toronto, Canada. © Lynne Knowlton | TreeHouse & Cabin Retreat.

p.255 A-Frame Wandawega: Woods of Wisconsin, USA. © Bennett Young.

ACKNOWLEDGEMENTS

First of all, thank you to everyone who took the time to journey through this collection of small spaces from all over the world. I hope that a sense of freedom to escape the norm and pursue something greater has been instilled within you.

A big thank you to the whole team at Ebury Press: my fantastic editor, Elen Jones. From vision to reality, your creativity, well-rounded experience and passion to see this come to life set the course to make it the remarkable book that it is today. Louise McKeever and Laura Marchant for your close help, thorough guidance and encouragement throughout.

Therese Vandling, for designing a beautiful collection to venture through.

Thank you to all the tiny house owners and builders for giving us an invitation into the extraordinary dwellings you call home – Daniel Norris, Matt Impola, Ann Voskamp and many more.

A special thank you to the talented photographers of the homes featured here, James Barkman, Max Ablicki, Zac Ruiz and so many more. Your creative work has been the backbone of this stunning collection.

I couldn't have done this without supportive family and friends. So thank you to my parents, siblings and Cody, Harmonie and Jolene, for giving wisdom and feedback at any time.